Bedwetting and Accidents Aren't Your Fault

Why potty accidents happen and how to make them

Don't worry. We'll get it all fixed!

STOP

Written by

Steve Hodges, M.D.,
& Suzanne Schlosberg

Illustrated by Cristina Acosta

Acknowledgments

Thank you all so much!

We are immeasurably grateful to artist Cristina Acosta, whose clever and upbeat illustrations brought our ideas to life in vivid color. Brilliant!

Our hardworking and talented graphic designer, Dyan Roth, did a beautiful job, as always. And our excellent photographer, Gary Alvis, worked at the speed of light. Thank you, Nancy Kruh, for reviewing the book with a fine-tooth comb.

So many families contributed to this book without knowing it, simply by sharing their stories with us and asking wise questions. Insights from Kathy Steinert and Angela Villalobos led directly to certain illustrations, as did ideas from Ian and Toby Spencer.

On a more fundamental level, we are grateful to Dr. Sean O'Regan, whose impeccable studies provide the scientific foundation to the concepts explained in this book and in *The M.O.P. Book*.

BedwettingAndAccidents.com

Bedwetting and Accidents Aren't Your Fault, 3rd Edition
Text Copyright © 2017 Steve J. Hodges and Suzanne Schlosberg
Illustration Copyright © 2017 Cristina Acosta
Book design: DyanRothDesign.com

O'Regan press

Library of Congress Cataloging-in-Publication Data is available on file.

ISBN: 978-0-9908774-6-2

Bedwetting and Accidents Aren't Your Fault

Written by

Steve Hodges, M.D., & Suzanne Schlosberg

Illustrated by

Cristina Acosta

This book is
dedicated to

Stella Grace,
Abigail, and
Rose Hodges
&
Toby and Ian
Spencer

What's Inside

PLUS A poop chart to hang in your bathroom!

Accidents are never a kid's fault!

Did you know millions of kids have accidents?

All over the world, kids have **pee** accidents at school, on the playground, and at home.

Many kids have **poop** accidents, too. Their poop falls out, and they don't even **feel** it.

Most of my patients wake up at **night** with wet sheets.

4

Sometimes adults wonder if kids have accidents on **purpose**. But kids don't, of course!

Accidents are a little like sneezes. You know how, when your nose gets tingly, you can't hold back that ah-choo?

Same with accidents:
They just happen — and fast!

But here's how accidents are **different** from sneezes: **Over time**, you can **train** your body to make them stop.

Mrs. Zipper, right now Zack and Zoe can't stop their accidents. Their insides have gone a little nutty.

MoM! MY tummy hurts...

The lump gives some kids a **stomachache**.

The poop pile-up happens in a stretchy tube called your colon — and especially at the end of your colon, called your **rectum**.

The poop pile hardens and **stretches** your rectum, like a rat stretches a snake's belly.

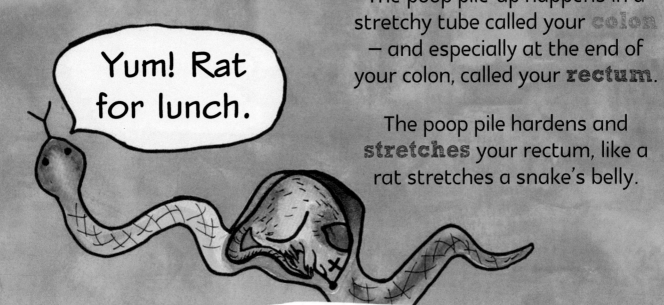

Yum! Rat for lunch.

When the lump gets big enough,
it squishes your bladder.

The bladder is **stretchy**, like a balloon, and it has a hole at the bottom where your pee comes out.

Imagine if you **squeezed** a water balloon that had a tiny hole in it! The water would **leak** out — like when you have a pee accident or wet your bed.

12

Healthy Colon   # Floppy Colon

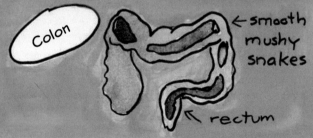

How do poop accidents happen?

Well, that poop **lump** can stretch your rectum so much that the rectum becomes floppy, the way your shirt will get floppy if you **stretch** it over your knees.

A **floppy** rectum can't keep in all your poop. So, some of it just drops out your bottom.

Plus, when your **rectum** is stretched, you can't always feel when poop needs to come out. So, even more **piles** up.

Oh no! She doesn't know her floppy rectum is dropping out a poop trail.

Let's imagine a giant **hairball** is clogging your family's bathtub. Will that **clog** go away if you sit around and wait?

Waiting won't work. Time to call for help!

Zack, how long do you think we need to wait for the drain to unclog itself?

I don't know Zoe. It sure is taking a long time.

Giant hairball in the bathtub plumbing

15

Of course not! You have to **clean** that hairball out of your pipe.

Same with your body: To make accidents **stop**, you have to clean that hard lump of poop out of your rectum — and keep your rectum **clear** every day.

Then, your rectum can **shrink** back to its normal size and stop squishing your bladder.

When your poop is soft

and squishy, it will **plop** out of your bottom without hurting.

To help clean out the lump, you may need to
take medicine that makes poop **mushy**.

Something else will also help
break up that poop lump: enemas.

Enemas do a super job!

You'll take off your undies and lie on your side
with your knees bent. Mom or Dad will let
water into your bottom through a **small** tube.

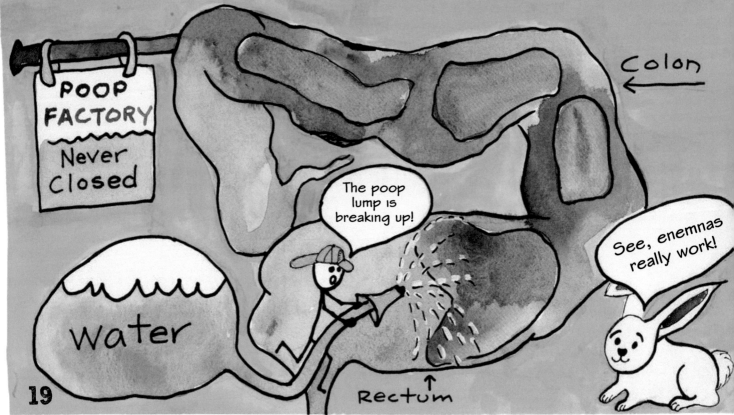

The **gentle** spray of water will loosen and **soften**
the poop, the way water streaming from a hose
can turn a **hard clump** of dirt into mud.

You'll try to **hold in** the enema for 5 to 10 minutes, but that
can take practice. Don't worry if you can't hold it that long.
Then you'll sit on the toilet and have a large poop.
You'll feel so much **better**!

Once your rectum is unclogged, it's important to

keep your poop soft so it doesn't get stuck

again and pile up.

Medicine will help. So will drinking plenty of **water**, staying really **active**, and eating lots and lots of **fruits** and **vegetables**.

Some foods — like mac and cheese, chicken nuggets, and potato chips — will make your poop **hard**. So, don't eat foods like these often!

Eat lots of fruits and vegetables.

Drink plenty of water.

Run and jump and play soccer and dance!

22

Also, keep pooping — a lot!

After **breakfast** and after **dinner**, sit on the toilet and give your poop a chance to come out.

Stay on the toilet for a full **five** minutes.

Read a book or play a game. Setting a **timer** can help, too.

Don't hop off the potty!

POOP CHART WINNERS

Long Thin Snakes   Mushy Blobs

Keeping your colon **clear** will definitely help you stay dry.

But you have one other important job: peeing a lot.

Frequent peeing **helps** your bladder
stay big, stretchy, and healthy.

But if you **hold in** your pee, your bladder will go nutty.
It might **hiccup** and spurt pee when you're not near a toilet

When your body tells you it's time to pee, go to the bathroom – even if you are at school.

Don't cross your legs or squeeze your private area to keep pee inside!

One more thing!

Every time you poop, tell your mom or dad what your poop looks like.

If it looks hard, like rabbit **pellets**, a **log**, or a bumpy **sausage**, your rectum is still clogged.

But if your poop looks like thin snakes or mushy blobs, you're all clear.

Hang this **poop chart** in your bathroom as a reminder!

WOW!
I pooped out a thin garden snake!

I knew he could do it!

About the Authors

Suzanne Schlosberg

Suzanne is a health and parenting writer who specializes in translating clinical mumbo jumbo into stuff that's fun to read. Years ago, on a mission to achieve a diaper-free household, Suzanne potty-trained her twin boys too early; she used Steve Hodges' methods to undo the damage. The author or co-author of 18 books and countless articles, Suzanne runs BedwettingAndAccidents.com and O'Regan Press. Her website is SuzanneSchlosbergWrites.com. Suzanne lives with her husband and boys in Bend, Oregon.

Steve Hodges, M.D.

Steve Hodges is an associate professor of pediatric urology at Wake Forest University School of Medicine and an expert in bedwetting, constipation, and potty training. He has authored numerous journal articles and co-authored five books with Suzanne Schlosberg. His mission is to shed light on the childhood constipation epidemic and to communicate to families that bedwetting and accidents are never a child's fault. Dr. Hodges lives in Winston-Salem, North Carolina, with his wife and three daughters. He blogs at BedwettingAndAccidents.com.

About the Artist

Cristina Acosta

Cristina is a painter and designer known for her lyrical artistry and bold use of color — and, these days, her clever take on childhood constipation. The author and illustrator of *Paint Happy* and illustrator of *When Woman Became the Sea*, Cristina also illustrates all the books and content for BedwettingAndAccidents.com. Cristina has taught painting and drawing and also designs home decor. Though Cristina's daughter is long past potty accidents, Cristina is excited to help children grow up confident and healthy. divides her time between Palm Springs, California, and Bend, Oregon. Her website is CristinaAcosta.com.

The Story Behind the Story
Information for Parents, Educators, and Medical Professionals

Q&A

with Steve Hodges, M.D.
Associate professor of pediatric urology at Wake Forest University School of Medicine

Bedwetting and Accidents Aren't Your Fault is based on the approach to treating toileting troubles detailed in *The M.O.P. Book: A Guide to the Only Proven Way to STOP Bedwetting and Accidents*. Here, Dr. Hodges briefly explains the scientific foundation for his approach and answers questions he is commonly asked. For details, go to BedwettingAndAccidents.com

Q: Aren't accidents a normal part of childhood?

A: That's a myth. Accidents are common, but that's only because constipation is common. In potty-trained children, bedwetting and accidents almost always signal a stuffed rectum and a bladder gone haywire. Children who never quite graduate to fully toilet trained or who continue to have accidents well after training typically aren't "late bloomers" or "rebellious"; they're chock full of poop.

Q: How can you be sure bedwetting and accidents are caused by constipation?

A: The connection is well documented in the scientific literature and confirmed daily in my practice. The most rigorous studies were led by Sean O'Regan, M.D., a kidney specialist whose 5-year-old son wet the bed. The boy's rectum was so stretched by stool, tests showed, that he couldn't detect a tangerine-sized air balloon inflated in his bottom.

Ultimately, Dr. O'Regan's research team tested hundreds of children with enuresis (pee accidents), encopresis (poop accidents), and recurrent urinary tract infections. Virtually all their rectums were stuffed with poop. After an enema regimen lasting several weeks, their accidents and infections stopped. I discuss this research in *It's No Accident* and *The M.O.P. Book*.

In my own practice, X-rays show well over 90 percent of patients with toileting problems are severely constipated. Often the stool mass is so large it stretches the rectum to twice its normal diameter and flattens the bladder. When these children follow an enema protocol similar to Dr. O'Regan's, accidents resolve. There's just no question constipation was the culprit.

Yum! Rat for lunch.

Q: But don't some kids wet the bed because they are deep sleepers or have small bladders?

A: Deep sleep cannot explain why a child's bladder would be overactive at 3 a.m. Children with healthy bladders simply should not need to empty overnight. Most kids are deep sleepers; most kids do not pee in the middle of the night. When my patients' rectums are cleaned out, they stop wetting the bed, despite being "deep sleepers." Some kids do wet the bed because their bladders are small, but that's because a mass of stool is flattening the bladder — not because the bladder is "underdeveloped."

Q: How about stress — doesn't that play a role in bedwetting and accidents?

A: On the whole, stress doesn't cause accidents, but accidents can absolutely cause stress. Children who wet the bed or poop in their pants may get teased by their peers, even shamed by adults, and generally feel crummy because they cannot control their bodies. So it's not surprising many of them display "difficult" behavior. These kids are often referred by schools or doctors to behavioral therapists when their problems are physiological, not psychological. When a child is just learning to use the toilet, anxiety related to the arrival of a new sibling or starting a new school may contribute to accidents. But once a child is toilet trained, what appears to be "regression" is more typically a progression — of constipation.

Q: How can I be sure a child is constipated?

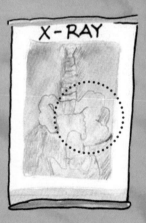

A: If the child wets the bed or has daytime accidents, you can generally assume the child is chronically constipated. Other red flags: giant bowel movements, poops resembling rabbit pellets or logs, recurrent UTIs, belly pain, the frequent or urgent need to pee, and pooping multiple times a day. Doctors who simply feel a child's abdomen and ask about pooping frequency will miss most cases of constipation. A severely constipated child can poop daily and have a belly that looks and feels normal. If there's any question, an X-ray will provide proof. A rectum wider than 3 cm indicates constipation; most children with wetting problems have rectums stretched to 6 or 7 cm in diameter.

Q: Is it safe to X-ray a child for constipation?

A: Yes. The radiation dose of an abdominal X-ray is the same dose you get from simply living for three months. The amount of good you can do for a child by accurately diagnosing constipation far outweighs the risks of a couple of plain X-rays. Broken legs — for which nobody questions X-rays — heal in six weeks; undiagnosed constipation can cause years of suffering. So while an X-ray isn't necessary to detect constipation, it can provide tangible evidence that the accidents are in no way the child's fault. An X-ray also can catch the unusual cases where constipation is not the cause of wetting. On occasion accidents are caused by type 1 diabetes, neurological problems, or an anatomical blockage of the bladder.

32

Q: At what age do you recommend taking action if a child is wetting the bed?

A: Age 4. Bedwetting that seems "developmental" often can be fixed fairly easily, saving families from lost sleep, stress, and unnecessary expense. Don't wait until a child is 7! Though many children do outgrow bedwetting, others do not. I have many teenage patients whose bedwetting was dismissed for years.

Q: Which works better for resolving accidents: laxatives or enemas?

A: Enemas — by far., although a combination works best. Osmotic laxatives such as Miralax, magnesium citrate, and lactulose suffice when a child is constipated but not having accidents. However, when constipation is so severe as to cause accidents or bedwetting, the most reliable fix is a daily enema regimen.

I call this regimen M.O.P., the Modified O'Regan Protocol — named after the three-month enema regimen Dr. O'Regan used in his numerous published studies. I have "modified" the regimen by adding a daily dose of osmotic laxative and making a few other adjustments. *The M.O.P. Book* spells out the protocol in great detail.

In a published study of 60 children with daytime wetting, my clinic compared M.O.P. with standard treatment — laxatives, a pee schedule, and, in some cases, bedwetting medication. After three months, 30% of the patients treated with standard therapies had stopped wetting. In the enema group, 85% of the patients were dry. X-rays showed that the children who were still wetting remained constipated despite the daily enemas. For tough cases like these, I recommend M.O.P.+, a more aggressive regimen also described in *The M.O.P. Book*.

Q: Can bedwetting medication help?

A: I don't recommend medication for resolving bedwetting. Medication can trick the kidneys into making less urine at night, but when the child stops taking the drug, the bedwetting typically returns. Medication doesn't fix the problem but rather covers it up.

Q: What about bedwetting alarms?

A: If a child wets the bed but does not have daytime accidents, an alarm can be helpful — but only if the child is also being treated aggressively for constipation. An alarm is not a substitute for bedwetting treatment, since it does not address the root of the problem. However, an alarm can train a child to wake up before wetting the bed.

Q: Aren't the kids in the book too old to be using a toilet stool?

A: Absolutely not! Children of all ages, especially those struggling with constipation, should poop with their feet on a stool to mimic the squatting position. (Adults should, too!) Fact is, humans were designed to squat. Squatting straightens the rectum, letting poop fall out easily — no straining! Anyone who's camped in the woods knows this. As I explain in *The M.O.P. Book*, research proves squatting makes pooping faster and easier. By contrast, sitting upright is like trying to poop uphill: With the rectum bent, poop has a tougher exit. What's more, toilets are too tall for children. With their feet dangling, kids often clench their inner thighs and can't relax. The stool illustrated in our book is the Squattypottymus, a children's version of the Squatty Potty. Though I am paid to endorse the Squattypottymus, I think any stool tall enough to place the child in a squatting position will do the job.

Q: Why are constipation, bedwetting, and accidents so common?

A: I see three main reasons: 1.) the highly processed Western diet, 2.) toilet training too early, and 3.) restrictive school bathroom policies.

1.) Diet: The same highly processed, low-fiber diet that contributes to the childhood obesity epidemic also causes stool to become firm and pooping to become painful. Many babies become constipated upon starting solids, and poop piles up from there. Also, some children appear to develop constipation due to food intolerances, especially to dairy.

2.) Early toilet training: Preschool potty-training requirements prompt many parents to train their children as toddlers. Problem is, 2-year-olds don't have the judgment to respond to their bodies' urges in a timely manner. So, many of them develop the holding habit. My published research shows children trained before age 2 have triple the risk of developing wetting problems than children trained later. Based on my clinical experience, I do not advise training until around age 3.

3.) Restrictive school bathroom policies: Some 36% of elementary teachers encourage holding by rewarding students who don't use bathroom passes or punishing those who do, according to a University of California at San Francisco survey. Fully 76% of teachers implement policies that undermine their students' toileting health. In addition to restrictive school bathroom policies, the unclean state of many school restrooms discourages students from using the bathroom at school.

Want to know more? Go to BedwettingAndAccidents.com or buy *The M.O.P. Book*.

Download Our FREE Infographics
BedwettingAndAccidents.com

When to X-ray a Child for Constipation

9 Kid-Tested Ways to Make Enemas Less Scary

The K-12 Teacher's Fact Sheet on Childhood Toileting Troubles

12 Signs Your Child is Constipated

Bedwetting: 4 Truths Every Parent Should Know

4 MiraLAX Facts You Didn't Know

Praise for Our Other Books

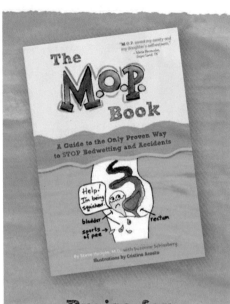

Praise for The M.O.P. Book

"It is my mission to get the word out about how incredibly effective M.O.P. is."

– Erin Wetjen, PT, specialist in pediatric incontinence Mayo Clinic, Rochester, MN

"M.O.P. saved my sanity and my daughter's self-esteem."

– Marta Bermudez, Sugar Land, TX

"M.O.P. stopped the constant accidents and allowed my child to live a normal life."

– Verified Amazon purchaser

Praise for Jane and the Giant Poop

"A must-read for grown-ups, too!"

– Sally Kuzemchak, R.D., RealMomNutrition.com

"Very cute & engaging book. My kids read it 3 times first day it arrived. Helped "normalize" their issue and bring humor to the process we are experiencing."

– Verified Amazon purchaser

"Terrific! The illustrations and humor are priceless."

– Angelique Champeau, CPNP, Director, Pediatric Continence Clinic UCSF Benioff Children's Hospital, Oakland and San Francisco

Praise for Dr. Pooper's Activity Book

"A great resource for kids with constipation and potty accidents! It helps them talk about it without embarrassment and understand and resolve their problems."

– Mike Garrett, M.D.Family Physician Direct MD, Austin TX

"Engages both parents and children to be aware of their bowel and bladder habits in a fun way. I will definitely recommend this book to my patients."

– James Sander, MD Clinical Assistant Professor of Urology Medical University of South Carolina

Made in the USA
Lexington, KY
11 June 2018